BRITISH SAWS

A History and Collector's Guide

Simon Barley

AMBERLEY

First published 2016

Amberley Publishing
The Hill, Stroud
Gloucestershire, GL5 4EP

www.amberley-books.com

Copyright © Simon Barley, 2016

The right of Simon Barley to be identified as
the Author of this work has been asserted in
accordance with the Copyrights, Designs and
Patents Act 1988.

ISBN 978 1 4456 4974 0 (print)
ISBN 978 1 4456 4975 7 (ebook)

British Library Cataloguing in Publication Data.
A catalogue record for this book is available from
the British Library.

Typesetting by Amberley Publishing.
Printed in the UK.

Contents

Acknowledgements

In the seventeen years since Ken Hawley asked me to catalogue the saws in his collection, much of what I have learned until his death in 2014 has been either directly from him, or from the unparalleled range of objects, catalogues and documents he put together. I owe a huge amount to him, his foresight and his perspicacity in knowing, against what most other people would just throw away, which things were going to add to the picture of Sheffield industry until it began to fade away in the last thirty years of the twentieth century. It is therefore in recognition of the importance of Ken and the Ken Hawley Tool Collection Trust that royalties from the sale of this book will go into the funds that maintain this collection.

There are of course many others besides him, the Onlie Begetter, who have helped me to understand how saws were made and marketed, used, repaired and resold as collectables. The list that follows is not in order of importance or significance, and I hope that those omitted will remember that their help is nonetheless always appreciated; I thank them all, although there will be some who are more aware than others how heavily I have leaned on their knowledge and good will: Jane Rees, the late Jay Gaynor, David Millett, Fred Storer, Geoff Tweedale, John Collier, Peter Barnes, Stephen Woodward, Hugh Thompson (who kindly read the book in an earlier draft), Richard Arnold, my fellow volunteers at the Hawley Collection (especially Gareth Morgan, who did with Photoshop what I could not, and Kate Hodgson, who also read the book and made many helpful comments), the contributors to www.backsaw.net (especially its originator Ray Gardiner), many dealers and collectors at the David Stanley auctions, members of the Tools and Trades History Society, and in the USA, among several others, Phil Baker, Mike Stemple and Vince Brytus (who generously repatriated rare British saws from their collections).

Picture credits

Sheffield Museums Trust for figure 12
Sheffield City Archives for figures 12 and 18
Bill Rypka for figure 8
Ted Ingraham for figures 10 and 11
Jane Rees for figure 94
Roald Renmælmo for figure 129
John Collier, of Monument Tools Plc, for figure 148
Vangelis Zournatzis Samios for figure 160
Thomas Flinn Saw Works for permission to take figures 50 and 51
Ray Gardiner for permission to modify figures 173 and 174
All other images are either from the Ken Hawley Tool Collection, or my own.

Why Collect British Saws?

Most people think they know what a saw looks like. In their mind it's an old tool, pretty rusty, hanging up in the shed or the garage with other similar cobwebby objects that hardly ever get used apart from being taken down for some occasional DIY. There are of course also those owned by a second group, the professional woodworkers, using mainly machines powered by small electric motors alongside a throwaway hand saw with a brightly coloured plastic handle.

But out there is also a very different person, on the obsessive side perhaps, who has not one saw but many, none of them with a cobweb and all clean, with the brass and wood looking as they might have done when they were made over a century ago. This book, written by someone who's an enthusiastic member of the last group, brings together information for those who are perhaps in the first but who might be tempted to change.

Maybe a saw in an auction or on a table at a car boot sale, or online with the hundreds always being offered; perhaps one of these has a name that catches the eye, or a decorative design on the blade, or is simply attractive because it combines history, function and beauty in the way that only a well-used tool can do.

1. Part of the author's saw collection at the Ken Hawley Tool Collection Trust in Sheffield.

2. This highly decorative saw was made by a Sheffield firm in about 1890.

3. The design on the 'Willow' saw also celebrates the firm's successes.

4. The design on the medallion screw also acknowledges its origins in the china industry.

There was nothing in the least romantic about the men (and they were almost without exception men) who made these tools, and the conditions under which they did so were unenviable, to say the least, offering as they did constant hard physical labour at piece-work rates, with the strong possibility of damage, even lethal, to their

5. A hand saw handle showing wear from the user's hand.

health. The products of their immense skill were then sold to craftsmen (again, few were female) who had to spend substantial sums of money to acquire the tools of their trade, carefully maintaining them and leaving on them marks of usage that signal the hundreds of hours of work with which they kept themselves alive and fed their families.

A saw might cost the equivalent of two weeks' wages, so marking it with one's name was a sign of pride, and a wise move in a world where portable property was so often removed for illegal resale.

What follows is some history and some practical advice, aimed at preserving – for use as well as the sheer pleasure of collecting – the products of our ancestors, and some of the tools and artefacts related to saws themselves. Of the many millions that were made, there are still thousands to be acquired: I hope that the information here will make the collecting and the preservation both discriminating and pleasurable.

6. The name struck on a saw handle always signifies an owner, not the maker.

The British Saw Industry: A Brief History

Although the saw is one of the oldest tools used by humans, an industry to make them in England did not begin until the late sixteenth century. The first English saw makers of whom much is known were a three-generation family called White, who worked on the edge of the city of London between 1650 and 1750 (for details, see Bibliography). Their saws became the most desirable and expensive on both sides of the Atlantic, but only two of their saws are known to have survived: both were found, and remain, in the eastern United States.

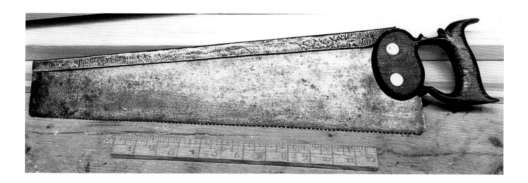

Above: **8.** A back saw made in London about 1750. (Courtesy of Bill Rypka)

Right: **9.** Above his name, the maker's mark on the previous saw shows a crown, a frequently used symbol that suggests quality.

Saws of the later eighteenth century by other makers are similarly rare, with perhaps fewer than 200 known worldwide. It is not possible to lay down more than the broadest of principles about their appearance, but it is worth doing so because they do still turn up from dusty workshops and outhouses, and to chance upon one of these rarities is an excitement so seldom enjoyed that it is as well to know what to look for.

The Whites made their saws in London, then the largest manufacturing city in the world, and with a population of 600,000 by far the biggest city, and port, in Britain. The range of trades in London was also immense, as the numbers of its wealthy inhabitants and the worldwide reach of its export trade put huge levels of demand into the demand/supply equation. But just as today the price of houses in London makes prices rise elsewhere in the country, so the stimulus of metropolitan markets spread to the provinces.

The next place to start a saw-making industry was Birmingham, where the metal trades had had a major home since the Middle Ages; by the 1760s there were probably a dozen men making saws there, some specialising completely, some combining this new trade with their older one of making edge tools.

10. A back saw made by Dalaway in Birmingham in about 1770. (Courtesy of Ted Ingraham)

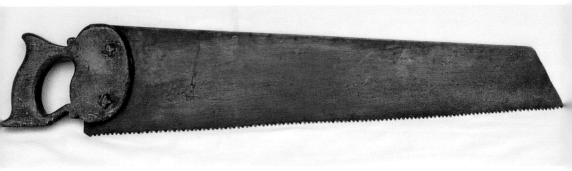

11. A hand saw by the same Birmingham maker from about 1770. (Courtesy of Ted Ingraham)

A few days' horseback ride away to the north was another ancient town of metalworkers, Sheffield, whose knives and other cutting-edge tools were mentioned by Chaucer in the fourteenth century and which took on saw making in the 1750s (see figure 12), to become the world centre of the trade for the subsequent 100 years.

Why should Sheffield have become so important in British saw making? This town – smaller than Birmingham, remote in its steep valleys, with no canals, no railways, not even a good road out – was the place where the two most important elements in saw making were harnessed: steel, and the water power to work it. The fact that there was no tradition of saw making was only briefly a handicap, as the town's prosperous entrepreneurs were soon able to buy in skilled labour from London and Birmingham.

The important parts of the saw are the blade and the handle. Once humans began metalworking, the choice for the blade was determined partly by what metal was available and partly by what worked best. The one that became known as steel has a long history, and a very complicated one. The ingredients which give it its unique properties are iron and carbon (until stainless forms were invented about 100 years ago); varying the proportions of the two elements only slightly makes large changes to the properties of the steel, so that different kinds can be specified for different purposes. The illustration (figure 13) shows labels taken from the bars of the many kinds of bespoke steel that a Sheffield firm could supply in about 1900.

Iron Age people probably achieved the occasional manufacture of steel by accident when a lump of their iron was overheated for a long time with charcoal (i.e. carbon), making a sort of steel on the surface of the metal. Later, this process was called case hardening, and could be deliberately done to make a material that would form a better tool. Making true steel was much more difficult, but again, metalworkers gradually found that they could get their iron hotter and in India even managed to melt it in very small quantities in clay pots, the resulting highly prized metal being called Wootz steel, which was exported globally and used particularly for swords.

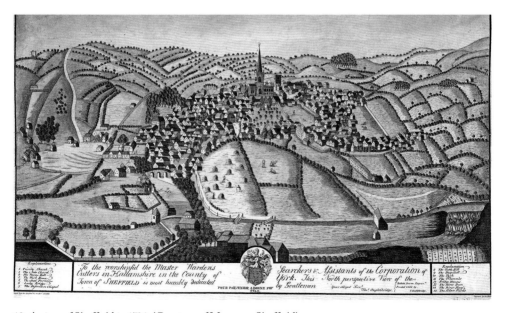

12. A view of Sheffield in 1736. (Courtesy of Museums Sheffield)

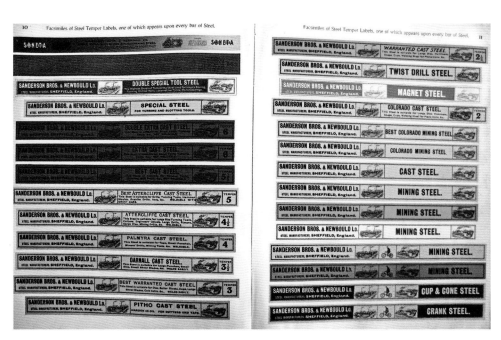

13. A partnership agreement of 1757 setting up Sheffield's first business in the 'Art, Trade or Mistery of Saw making' (line 11). (Courtesy of Sheffield City Archives)

14. Labels on steel bars from a Sheffield steel maker's catalogue of 1900.

Other ironworkers, lacking the capacity to melt the iron, simply reheated their carbonised material in a furnace and by hammering it, bending and folding it for further hammering, mixed the harder material on the surface with the softer, less carbonised iron beneath. The results of this kind of forging were, and are, steels of very high quality, and metalworkers worldwide have perfected the techniques; cities like Toledo or Damascus gave their names to products much sought after for swords and tools, and Japanese steels made in this way are equally legendary. In England techniques of steel making were imported from Germany in the seventeenth century, arriving first in north-eastern counties and later spreading to Birmingham, Sheffield, London and elsewhere.

As far as English saws are concerned, the greatest advance in steel making came in the middle of the eighteenth century from the work of a Sheffield clockmaker called Benjamin Huntsman, who was dissatisfied with the quality of the steel he was using for watch springs. He was familiar with techniques of melting brass for clock parts, and spent several years experimenting with clay crucibles and steel mixtures before he achieved a replicable process for a melted steel that could be cast into small ingots. When reheated and forged for tools, this steel became one of the best in the world and made the name famous for ever.

When Sheffield men started to produce saws in 1757, these were extremely complex tools to make. First a piece of steel in ingot or bar form had to be made red hot, before being rolled into a flat sheet, which then underwent more than a dozen processes of cutting to shape, punching out the teeth, hardening and tempering, hammering on an anvil to make it as flat as possible ('smithing'), and grinding on a large grindstone.

Then followed further hammering to ensure the blade was correctly 'tensioned' (so that it would return to straight after bending), heating, polishing, fitting the wooden handle, and ending with the teeth being sharpened and set with a hammer (see also figures 49 and 50).

The knowledge and skills used in this manufacture were so specialised that soon tradesmen had differentiated themselves into grinders, smithers, handle makers and so on, and by the 1820s there were about 400 men in the Sheffield industry; the 1841 national Census showed that four in five of all the saw makers in England and Wales worked in that one town, a proportion that did not change until the industry

15. Sheffield saw grinders in the mid-nineteenth century.

contracted to today's very small numbers. Closely linked to saw making were the allied industries of steel and file making; the largest Sheffield firms often had each of these trades under their own roof, thus ensuring the high quality of the raw material and the essential saw/sawfile pairing.

By 1850 the industrial economy of Britain was the largest and most productive in the world, its factories supplying goods not only to its empire of colonies but also to other continents where Britain's early lead in mass production had not yet been challenged. Saw making was concentrated in Sheffield, which was able to draw together its advantages in crucible cast steel making, local raw materials like grindstones and coke for the furnaces, its specialised labour force with its powerful traditions of skills passed from father to son, and its networks of manufacturers in other metal manufactures – all combining to create an industrial atmosphere almost unparalleled anywhere in the world. The small business that the Kenyon brothers had started in 1757 became by the end of the next century just one of several huge establishments which every year could turn out tens of thousands of saws, files, steel and other tools.

Saw manufacturers sold their goods to the hundreds of ironmongers and tools retailers across the country, marking saws with the shopowner's name.

The export trade was dealt with in the same way, with beautiful designs etched on saws that went in their thousands to all parts of the world.

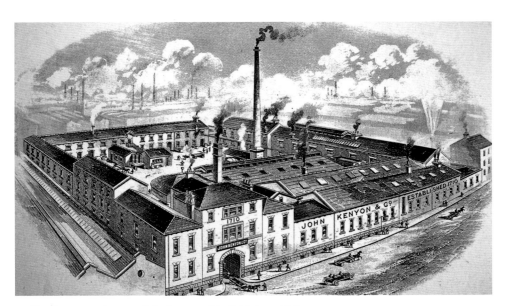

16. The Kenyon steel, saw and file factory in Sheffield about 1910.

17. A saw made for a retailer; note the owner's name added (with a mark punch not intended for metal, hence the letters are less deep).

We pay particular attention to packing; each Saw is put in a separate envelope cover, and all are boxed in ⅓ dozens. Lots of 12 dozen and upwards, we will, if desired, etch with Customer's Name in addition to our name and Corporate Mark, and the words "Made for."

List of discounts on application.

We are, Dear Sirs,

Yours faithfully,

RICHARD GROVES & SONS, LTD.

18. Part of the preface to the 1915 Groves catalogue.

19. The design etched on saws exported by Taylor Brothers of Sheffield in the 1870s (a steel plate for printing etching transfers). (Courtesy of Sheffield City Archives)

It is important to remember that the Sheffield saw trade produced its tools in several different qualities; these differences reflected the amount of work put into making the steel blade better and to decorating and finishing the handle. The largest firms sold at least five qualities, the best – more than twice as expensive as the cheapest – often described as 'Warranted London Spring'. Some firms, for instance Taylor Brothers, simply attached completely different brand names (see figure 159). Another instance is the brand 'John Cockerill', which was a second quality product line of Spear & Jackson. The word 'London' was often put on Sheffield-made saws to add a suggestion of high quality (see figure 168).

As well as decorating the saw blade, manufacturers attracted the buyer's eye with a decorative medallion screw. Scores of different ones were made, usually individual to the firm and bearing its trade mark, although the most commonly found are those with the words 'Warranted Superior'. A few examples are shown; a complete and international range can be found at www.backsaw.net. No examples of medallions specific to London or Birmingham makers have been recorded.

The world war that started in 1914 brought increased production of Sheffield saws and tools of all kinds, with many saw firms also making steel for armaments (see figures 43 and 44).

In spite of the wartime boom, however, by 1918 the British economy was almost on its knees, and saw manufacturers could not escape the slump of the following decade, in which many firms ceased production. In Sheffield the Kenyons, who for 150 years had concentrated on export to Russia, found that the Communist government there had neither the will nor the cash to pay, and by 1930 were bankrupt (although to their astonishment, their successor company was paid in part fifty years later).

And other factors were at work. Industrial progress in North America was on a scale that Britain could not match, and in Europe German manufacturers, who started later and could copy British successes but avoid their failures, put their superior educational methods into an industrial system that overtook many firms in fields far wider than the saw industry. New inventions such as electric motors became increasingly more efficient and better applied to new uses such as powering hand tools (see figure 45).

Modern business methods encompassed much more than manufacture: mass production by automated methods began to turn out larger numbers of tools more quickly and at a far lower price, and when the advertising skills of America were applied to selling these tools British firms were often left behind, even in colonies like Canada, Australia and New Zealand with long traditions of kinship and trading. The Philadelphia saw firm of Henry Disston, who had come from England in the 1840s, outsold the largest Sheffield makers and Disston even set up his own retail outlet in London in the 1870s: Disston's hard-selling methods to purvey cheaper but high quality saws were a devastating revelation to British saw makers.

20. 1820.

21. 1825.

22. 1850.

23. 1850.

24. 1860.

25. 1860.

26. 1860.

27. 1870.

28. 1870.

29. 1870.

30. 1880.

31. 1880.

32. 1880.

33. 1880.

34. 1880.

35. 1880.

36. 1880.

37. 1890.

38. 1890.

39. 1910.

40. 1920.

41. 1920.

42. 1930.

43. 1960.

A series of medallion screws from the earliest recorded up to the 1960s; the dating, as always with saws, is approximate. Numbers 24 and 29 were made for saws exported to the USA. All shown are about 1 inch in diameter, although on back saws they were usually about ¾ inch. The 'Warranted Superior' design of numbers 37, 42 and 43 was widely used by makers everywhere, even though some of its motifs, the crossed arrows, are adapted from the arms of the City of Sheffield.

44. The mark struck on a back saw made for the military in 1918.

45. This way of using a circular saw may have been even more dangerous than being exposed to enemy fire.

DR5GP

46. By 1960 electrically powered hand tools were well developed.

By the end of the twentieth century, sawing wood was almost entirely mechanised, from the saw mill where giant bandsaws reduce trees to sawn timber, down to the site joiner or carpenter who uses cheap, accurate, electrically powered saws for every job except an occasional cut with a throwaway, fast-cutting hand saw whose flame-hardened points were sharper than anything his father might have achieved with a file.

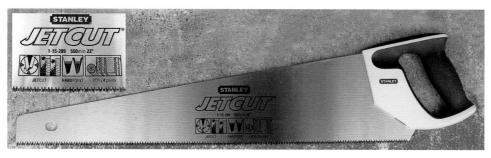

47. A modern hand saw, with plastic handle and fast cutting teeth (see detail).

48. A back saw of the same era.

Only at the bench of the cabinetmaker is there today much use of saws that need human muscle power, and although the old tools are highly valued, there is new competition in the form of saws made with tooth forms resembling the Japanese pattern, together with a few of the traditional types coming from a tiny number of surviving manufacturers, some literally one-man strong.

Nevertheless a measure of hand manufacture still goes on, chiefly by specialists who reproduce fine copies of old saws, but also in some of the firms which have survived all the vicissitudes of modern manufacturing.

49. A Japanese saw; there are many different types, all designed to cut on the pull stroke; the teeth on this one point backwards on one of the edges, the other being like the Jetcut teeth.

50. Hammer setting the teeth on a saw is still practised in Sheffield's Thomas Flinn saw works; see also figure 58.

51. Sharpening saw teeth by hand at the Thomas Flinn saw works; see also figure 58.

What to Collect

Whatever their interest – whether it is beer mats, lawn mowers, or saws – collectors collect what they consider collectable: objects that appeal to them in some way or other. This book will not lay down rules for choosing what is always a personal preference. The farmer with a spare barn may want nothing but pitsaws (see figures 128 and 129), always on the hunt for the bigger one, whereas the owner of a small flat might concentrate on what the Sheffield trade called toy saws, the miniature versions of hand and back saws that were often only a few inches long (see figures 53a and 53b).

Some collectors, often for reasons they cannot say, like to search out the products of a particular maker, perhaps attracted by family name. One friend prefers above all others the nineteenth-century Sheffield saws marked as made with German steel, which was an excellent steel that was cheaper than the highest quality crucible cast; it had nothing to do with Germany, and the name fell out of use by about 1910 (see figures 54 and 55).

In Sheffield's Central Library Archives there are business documents showing that even by the 1820s scores of different designs of saws were being sold from Sheffield, but this book does not have the space to consider all that were ever made; figures 56 and 57, from two Sheffield nineteenth-century catalogues, give an idea of some of the main types and the variations available.

*167
A 28 foot-saw used for cutting down Big Trees in California*

52. Saws used to fell giant redwoods in California were up to 28 feet long; British-made equivalents went more to Africa, Asia and Australasia.

53a. Nineteenth-century toy saws were probably made for children's tool kits.

53b. A group of toy saws 4–6 inches long; the bronze-bladed one was probably not made by a saw manufacturer.

54. Mark from a Sheffield-made saw of about 1840.

55. An advertisement of about 1890 by the maker of the saw in the previous illustration.

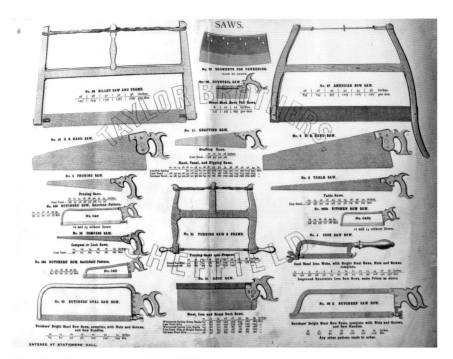

56. A plate from a catalogue of about 1890.

---

4   GROVE'S LIST OF PRICES.

Cast Steel Brass Back Saws.

No.		per doz.
	9 inches at	72s
60	10 do	72s
61	11 do	78s
62	12 do	80s
63	13 do	88s
64	14 do	90s
65	16 do	104s
66	18 do	112s
	20 do	120s

Cast Steel Turning Webs, or Bow Saws, Blue.

67	10 inches do	6s
68	11 do	7s
69	12 do	7s6d
71	14 do	9s
72	15 do	10s6d
73	16 do	11s6d
74	18 do	12s6d
75	20 do	15s
78	22 do	18s
77	24 do	20s
78	26 do	24s
	28 do	27s
79	30 do	30s
80	36 do	32s
		39s

Saw Webs, to Cut Iron, Brass, &c.

88	5 inches at	5s
89	6 do	6s
90	7 do	7s
91	8 do	8s
92	9 do	9s
93	10 do	10s
94	11 do	11s
95	12 do	12s

Cast Steel Ivory Saws, Blades blue or bright.
HALF INCH BROAD.

96	9 inches do	9s
97	15 do	10s
98	18 do	14s
99	21 do	18s
100	24 do	21s
101	26 do	24s
102	30 do	27s

WITH OR WITHOUT TEETH.

Cast Steel Ivory Saw Blades, blue or bright.
1 INCH BROAD.

No.		per doz.
103	12 inches at	12s
104	14 do	14s
105	16 do	16s
106	18 do	18s
107	20 do	20s
108	22 do	22s
109	24 do	24s
110	26 do	26s
111	28 do	28s
112	30 do	30s
113	32 do	32s
114	34 do	34s
115	36 do	36s

Cast Steel Ivory Saw Blades.
FROM 1 TO 1½ INCH BROAD.

116	12 inches at	18s
117	14 do	21s
118	16 do	21s
119	18 do	21s
126	20 do	30s
121	22 do	33s
122	24 do	36s

Cast Steel Ivory Saw Blades.
FROM 2 TO 2½ INCH BROAD.

123	26 inches at	39s
124	28 do	42s
125	30 do	45s
126	33 do	49s6d
127	36 do	51s
128	38 do	57s
129	40 do	60s

Thin Cast Steel Saw Blades.
NO TEETH.

No.	Long.	Broad.	Each
144	44 in.	4½ in. at	11s
145	49 do.	4½ do.	12s6d
146	54 do.	4½ do.	13s6d
147	55 do.	4½ do.	13s9d
148	60 do.	4½ do.	15s
149	66 do.	4½ do.	18s6d

SAWS.   5

Common Steel Pit, Frame, & Cross Cut Saws.

150	4 feet at	9s6d
151	4½ do	10s6d
152	5 do	11s6d
153	5½ do	12s6d
154	6 do	14s
155	6½ do	16s
156	7 do	18s
157	7½ do	21s
158	8 do	25s

German Steel Pit, Frame, and Cross Saws.

159	4 feet at	15s
160	4½ do	16s
161	5 do	18s
162	5½ do	19s6d
163	6 do	22s
164	6½ do	24s
165	7 do	26s
166	7½ do	30s
167	8 do	36s

Cast Steel Pit, Frame, and Cross Cut Saws.

168	4 feet at	16s6d
169	4½ do	17s6d
170	5 do	19s6d
171	5½ do	21s
172	6 do	24s
173	6½ do	26s
174	7 do	28s
175	7½ do	33s
176	8 do	39s
177	8½ do	41s
178	9 do	50s

If set and sharpened, 1s. 6d. each extra, all 11½ inches; but for 12 inches, 2s extra.

WARRANTED GOOD.
German Steel Mill Saws.

179	5 feet at	22s
180	5½ do	26s
181	6 do	28s
182	7 do	33s
183	7½ do	38s
184	8 do	44s

Cast Steel Mill Saws.

185	5 feet at	26s
186	5½ do	30s
187	6 do	30s
188	6½ do	37s
189	7 do	37s
190	7½ do	42s
191	8 do	48s

Cast Steel Span Saw Blades, Thin Fine Teeth.
FROM 1 TO 2 INCHES BROAD.

No.		per doz.
192	24 inches at	36s
193	27 do	48s6d
194	30 do	45s
195	33 do	49s6d
196	36 do	54s

Fret Saws, sorted.

No.		per doz.
From 4 to 10 inches at		5s
197	11 do	6s
198	12 do	7s
199	12 do double	10s

Cast Steel Hollow Scrapers.

No.	Length.	Broad.	doz.
200	6 inches by 2 at		8s

Square Scrapers.

201	6 inches by 2 at	6s
202	8 do	2	8s
203	10 do	2	10s
204	12 do	2	12s

Patent Iron Backed Currier Knives.

Complete .... 72s.
Spiral Cutters, any size, and Silver Steel Webs for Dressing Cloth.

57. Two pages from a saw maker's catalogue of 1840, showing the many varieties available.

The Hand Saw

This is what usually comes to mind as a 'saw': a tool with a steel blade 22–26 inches in length, toothed on one edge, and a wooden or perhaps nowadays a plastic closed handle. Below are the names of the most commonly found variations on this basic tool; in overall appearance they all look like the one in figure 59, but differ in size (length and width of the blade) and in the number and form of the teeth, the last usually expressed as points per inch.

	Length of blade (inches)	Points per inch
Rip saw	28–30	2½ – 3½
Half rip saw	26–28	4
Hand saw	22–26	5–7
Panel saw	20–24	6–11

Because they had different purposes, rip saws, which cut along the grain of the wood, had differently shaped teeth to saws designed to cut across it (for large cross-cut saws, with completely different tooth forms for green timber, see figure 127).

Many millions of hand saws have been made in the last 200 years, and used ones are easy to find. They were made in a vast range of different qualities and sizes. The most expensive, for the demanding professional, were given a high degree of individual finishing of both blade and handle, the material for this being perhaps rosewood or even ebony instead of the usual cheaper beech. For their top quality number 171 saw, Spear & Jackson in 1915 charged a *wholesale* price of 12 shillings and 9 pence each (roughly £45 in the money of 2015); even with a discount for the retailer on that price, his saw was often a woodworker's most expensive tool.

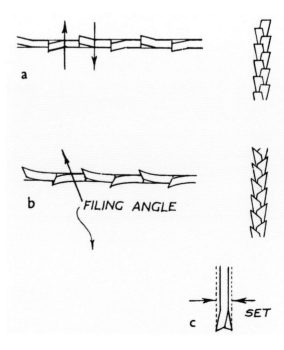

58. The different tooth forms of rip saws (a) and cross-cut saws (b); the filing and setting of teeth are shown in figures 49 and 50. (Adapted, with permission, from *Salaman's Dictionary of Woodworking Tools*)

59. This saw has an apple wood handle, possibly made in the USA for the Sheffield firm of Spear & Jackson.

For a really cheap saw that someone might buy for occasional use at home, the wholesale price was under 2 shillings each, and smaller saws, usually made in the grafting saw pattern, when supplied as part of a tool kit for the home were even less (see the illustrations of tool chests, 139–141). It may seem surprising to find that if these saws from the very bottom of the range are today cleaned up and well sharpened, they can perform quite satisfactorily on softwood.

Most hand saws were supplied with familiar looking teeth, but specially toothed ones were made for quick cutting of rough or green wood on the farm or in mines where propping of the roofs was with wooden timbers.

Of the several other types of hand saw, two can be mentioned. One was called a combination, or rule, saw, because it was etched with graduations along the back, and had a handle which doubled as a square. It continued in production until the 1970s. The other, called a docking saw, was copied from an American pattern, and was designed to withstand rough construction work outdoors. It was the only one with a metal handle, large enough for a user's gloved hand.

Many of these precious and expensive hand saws were used until they were worn out. Each sharpening removed metal until there was almost nothing left at the toe end. The collector may feel a sense of admiration for users who valued their saws to such an extent.

60. A 10-inch grafting saw ('grafter') of about 1900; the smallest are hard to distinguish from toy saws.

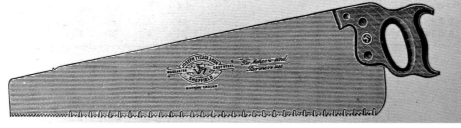

HAND SAW, AMERICAN LIGHTNING TOOTH
SPECIALLY SUITABLE FOR ROUGH WOOD

61. A saw sold for 'miners and farmers' in the 1920s; note the differently shaped teeth at the toe, known as incremental, or starter teeth, which make it easier to start the cut.

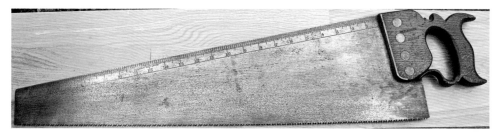

62. A rule, or combination, saw, made about 1880.

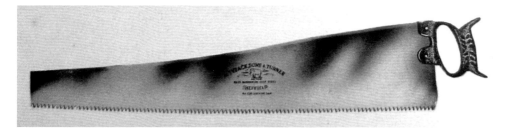

63. A docking saw; the handle shape is characteristic of this type only.

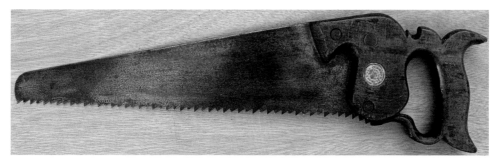

66. This saw, also from about 1870, has been sharpened very inexpertly, shortened and used almost to destruction.

64, 65. The blades of these saws of about 1870 show the results of many sharpenings, and wear on the handle from the user's hand, but the straightness of the tooth line has been preserved.

The design of the hand saw changed subtly over the years, and the collector can with practice easily see the difference, especially in the handles, between one made in the early nineteenth century and one made in the second half of the twentieth. The differences were based mainly on the steadily increasing use of machines to do what at first was all hand work. Although today some hand work remains in the finishing of a wooden saw handle, with the cutting out done by machine, it is not difficult to tell the difference between a saw handle of the 1970s and one of a century earlier (see figures 67 and 68).

The nineteenth-century industry in Sheffield was regulated by a joint committee of masters and men, setting piece-work rates that took account of the time needed to achieve the separate stages of manufacture – a system that went right across many more trades than saw making and in many more places than Sheffield. These rates of pay were sufficiently flexible to accommodate different levels of quality and advances in design. Figure 69 depicts two of the twelve pages from this 'statement', as it was called, of the prices paid to all saw handle makers in the Sheffield trade.

One major change in appearance came in the 1870s, when the American saw maker Henry Disston, an Englishman who emigrated in the 1840s and who eventually built up a business that became far larger than his largest British rivals, introduced a hand saw with what he called a skew back; in England it was sometimes called a hollow, or sway back (see figures 70 and 71). With this change to the elegant curving of the back of the blade, a decorative nib at the toe was no longer needed, and to add to Disston's fundamental rethinking of the balance of a saw, he introduced the 'let-in' handle, which aimed to increase the user's control of the sawing action.

67. The handle of this 1810 saw was entirely handmade.

68. Most the work on this 1970s handle was by machine.

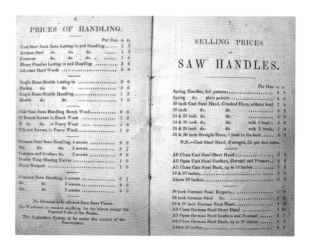

69. Two pages from the 'statement of prices' paid to saw handlemakers agreed in 1847.

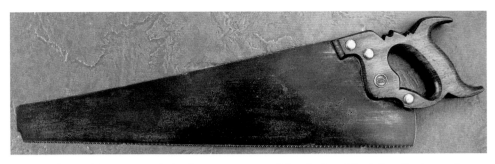

70. A hand saw of about 1910 with the American pattern of skew back and 'let-in' handle; the toe shows a small break.

As the next illustrations show, English firms like Joseph Tyzack quickly copied the new shape, but for decades on both sides of the Atlantic the two – straight and skew – continued to be produced.

As an aside, the matter of the decorative nib has to be mentioned: many uses for it have been proposed, but the true purpose, as stated in the handbook on saws produced by Spear & Jackson, Sheffield's oldest and largest firm, was purely decorative, words echoed in the similar handbook put out by Disston. Figure 74 is an example of a decorative nib was made on saws by Robert Sorby, a company with a very large trade with Australasia; their trademark was a kangaroo, and the decorated archway to their Sheffield works has been rebuilt as an entrance to the Ken Hawley Galleries at the Kelham Island Industrial Museum (figure 76).

Besides medallion screws, other decorative, perhaps semi-functional, features were 'register plates'. Made of brass with cast decorations (figure 77), or of flat iron or steel (figure 78), they were yet another feature which manufacturers could add to the range and give an edge to their competitiveness (see figures 77 and 78).

Given that apart from this one major change there was so little alteration in the appearance of the hand saw blade, the look of the handle is what shows any changes more easily. Figure 79 pictures a saw handle maker of the early twentieth century is probably somewhat romanticised (would 'Old Clegg' really have worn such a freshly creased apron for his everyday work?) and it is easy to see why there is nobody doing this kind of work in a modern saw factory.

71. A Sheffield skew back saw of about 1890.

72. Part of the etchings on the previous saw.

73. Straight backed saw, with nib, of the same period; the broken teeth are probably the result of over-zealous setting.

74. A nib of pure decoration.

Left: **75.** The same saw as figure 74, showing the multiple medallion screws which were often put on Sheffield saws made for export (see also figures 161–163).

Below: **76.** The arch from the former saw works of Robert Sorby in Sheffield.

77. The register plate from a Groves hand saw of about 1890; the beehive was one of the firm's trademarks.

78. A plain iron plate on a saw of about 1880.

79. The Sheffield saw handle maker 'Old Clegg', from a photograph of 1910.

The Back Saw

For several reasons, this type of saw survives better than the hand saw: although its blade is thinner, it has the extra strength of a folded rib of iron, steel or brass along the back; it was used for less heavy work and almost always in an indoor workshop, where a highly skilled and better paid man took greater care of it and used it for his most accurate work; as it needed sharpening less often, it remained useful for longer, and perhaps above all its combination of fine materials – polished steel and contrasting brass with a beautifully figured beech handle – made it something to value and be proud of.

This next example shows a much younger saw, made probably around 1900, but still, apart from some insignificant smudges of old rust on the blade, in fine condition: the blade is absolutely straight, and although a purist might want to touch up the teeth for optimum sharpness, it still cuts like a knife through butter, leaving a kerf a mere ¹⁄₆₄ inch wide.

In the eighteenth and nineteenth centuries, back saws bore different names depending on their length: dovetail (a 6 to 10-inch blade), carcass (10–14 inches), sash (14–16 inches) and tenon (16–20 inches); the term tenon saw is nowadays often loosely used for back saws of all these sizes.

Back saws were also made in a multitude of shapes, sizes and qualities; there is room here to mention only a few. The smallest toy saws had, as noted, a blade only 4 inches long, but even smaller were those made with a straight in-line handle known as gent's saws, used by hobbyists and in the jewellery trades (figure 83).

80. A 20-inch bladed saw made in about 1760, probably by Robert Jones for the Kenyon brothers, whose name it bears (see also their firm's indenture on p. 14).

81. An 8-inch back saw made by G. & T. Gray of Sheffield for Thomas Gardner, Bristol toolmakers and dealers.

82. A cut made by the Gray saw in the previous illustration.

83. A gent's saw with a 3½-inch blade, probably made about 1900, but saws looking exactly like this are still being made.

At the other end of the scale were saws intended to be used in special frames for mitreing door architraves, skirting boards and so on; these mitre-box saws were longer, up to 24 inches or more, and with a deeper blade. Other devices for sawing mitres used a saw with a web.

Other small back saws were made for different purposes, for instance the blitz saw for cutting metal, a German invention made also in Britain in the twentieth century. Another type was the small saw with its unique shape made for the electricity installer at a time when wiring was run in wooden casing (figure 87).

On smaller back saws, with blades up to 12 inches long, the handle was usually open. Until the early twentieth century most good quality back saws had prominent horns which not only contributed to the handsome appearance but, more importantly, helped to control the saw in use.

By about 1920 the design of the saw handles became progressively simpler, as machine manufacture gradually took over from the hand-made: there is little difficulty in seeing that the nineteenth-century elaborate touches to the handle of the Taylor Brothers' back saw had by about 1950 been cruelly modified under the influence of the machine (figure 93).

The back of a back saw often proved irresistible for owners to mark their possession, sometimes also with the date (figure 94). The buyer should beware, however, that any date whatever on a saw can be added at any time whatever, and can never be relied upon for dating its manufacture.

84. A mitre box made by the US firm Stanley, using a back saw.

85. A frame for sawing mitres, made about 1920; similar designs continue to be made.

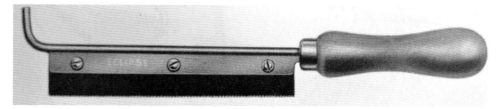

86. A blitz saw made in the 1950s, described by the makers as 'a useful saw for all slitting work and for small sawing jobs'.

87. An electrician's saw with a 3-inch blade from about 1920.

88. An 8-inch open-handled back saw made about 1820; as the next illustration shows, the design of this type of saw changed very little in almost a century.

89. An 8-inch back saw made about 1900 by a Sheffield firm for a Manchester tool dealer, whose name etched on the blade is still just visible.

90. A London-made saw of about 1930.

91. The London firm of Hazeon were abrasives makers, but sold many small back saws made for them between about 1930 and 1950.

92. See caption overleaf.

93. Two saws from early and late in the twentieth century by Taylor Brothers, one of Sheffield's largest and most innovative saw firms from 1837 to 1971.

94. A saw made in Sheffield, probably in the 1760s; Francis Keen was the owner, not the maker; this mark is on the reverse of the brass back.

Butchers' Saws

These were made in huge quantities and in many shapes and sizes. Some looked exactly like saws for woodworkers, but can often be distinguished if they have four screws securing the handle, as woodworkers' never had more than three. Butchers' saws were also frequently sold by firms which had their address in London's ancient meat market district, Smithfield. Some were labelled 'Kitchen Use'.

Other butchers' saws had, for obvious reasons, a stainless steel blade. For a few years (1930–50) stainless-steel-bladed back and hand saws were also made for woodworkers, but production did not continue as they did not perform as well as the usual steel saws; the collector may have to distinguish one use from another by the name on the saw.

The picture on p. 30 (figure 56) shows other types of butchers' saws; the most commonly found is illustrated below (figure 100) – note that butchers' saws have a characteristic handle, the forward edge being largely straight.

An unusual and unmistakeable type, called a chine saw, was used by two people to saw across the back (the 'chine') of a large animal (figure 101); American saws of this sort were called beef splitters.

95. A large, strong steel-backed butcher's saw of about 1930.

96. The mark on a Smithfield butcher's supplier's saw of about 1880.

97. A meat saw for 'kitchen use'; note the similarity to a woodworker's saw.

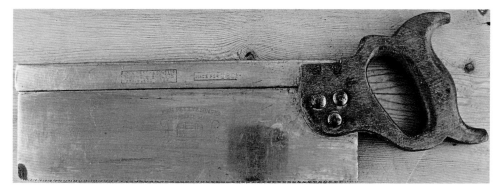

98a. A 12-inch stainless steel butcher's saw of about 1950.

98b. 'Made for DBC' (the Danish Bacon Company) reveals the purpose of the saw in the previous picture.

98c. This relatively faint image shows the difficulty of etching stainless steel, as does the next picture also.

99. Mark on a woodworker's back saw of about 1950.

100. Most saws made for butchers looked much like this one, made about 1910.

101. Two-man butcher's saw, marked as government property, 1942.

Saws for Cutting Metal

The oldest type of this category, nowadays called hack saws, was called a bow saw for iron, or Lancashire pattern. Examples from the eighteenth century are known. The design was going out of fashion in the early twentieth century, being superseded by varieties that were more easily adjustable, but they were made in enormous numbers and are often found.

A specialised type of saw that resembled a pruning saw (see p. 51) was made for plumbers, with one edge for cutting wood, the other, with finer teeth, for cutting metal, which at the date of the example shown would have been lead; the figures in the enlarged detail show the number of points per inch.

A blade for cutting metal was also usually included in nests of saws (see figure 114).

102. A bow saw for iron, made about 1880; the engineering industries of Lancashire used very large numbers of metal-cutting saws.

SPECIAL PLUMBERS' SAW, with two edges, one
to cut wood, the other for pipe, etc.,
Set and sharpened, S. & J.'s improved flat brass screws.

	16	18	20 inch.
No. 45 English beech handle, polished on edges	40/-	42/-	44/- doz.

Packed ⅓ doz. in a box.

Above: **103.** A plumber's saw from the Spear &
Jackson catalogue of 1915.

Left: **104.** The numbers struck on the blade
close to the handle indicate the number of
points per inch on the two edges.

Saws for the Garden

Usually known as pruning saws and, once again, of more different designs than can
be illustrated (figure 105). Those most often seen are toothed on both edges, like the
plumber's saw (figure 103), one with teeth known as 'lightning', which cut aggressively
in green wood, and with handles that are symmetrical; they were not high quality tools,
nor usually well looked after, as resinous and damp wood leave them corroded. Some
twentieth-century designs had curved blades, a design known as Grecian, or Australian
pattern; instead of a fixed wooden handle, some were made to have a long pole
inserted into a socket. The least often seen resembled a grafting saw. All were available
in different sizes. One unusual type was made only by Spear & Jackson (figure 106).

In recent times the blade could sometimes be made to fold into the handle or lock
into the working position; these saws are now made with very fast-cutting tooth
patterns in the Japanese style (see figure 46).

The two-edged pattern was in the nineteenth century issued to the guard of trains
in case of accidents, when it might have been necessary to cut passengers free of the
damaged wooden rolling stock (figure 109); similar saws were supplied for fire services
(figure 108).

105. The range of pruning saws offered by Robert Sorby (Sheffield) in 1935.

106. The 'Dawyck' pruner was offered in 1939, but did not reappear after 1945.

107. Modern folding pruning saw with Japanese-style teeth.

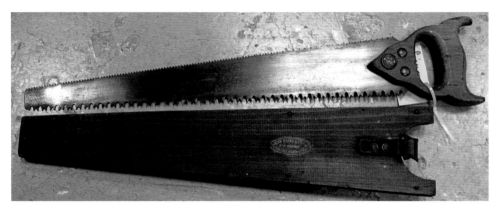

108. A pruning saw supplied by a Salford firm of 'fire engineers'.

109. A pruning saw (28-inch blade) supplied in around 1900 to the London & North Western Railway, which struck its initials deeply into the blade.

Frame Saws

All these saws use a narrow blade, called a web, held in tension; there is often a means for the blade to be rotated within the frame, either for curved work, or so as to gain access in awkward places. The frames were usually wood, but many types of metal-framed saws were developed in the twentieth century. The most commonly made was called a bow, turning, or sweep saw. Most European woodworkers used saws like this, often making their own frames; even today the usual hand saw beyond the Channel is one of these, often with a web up to 28 inches long.

Another frequently encountered type was called a buck saw, modelled after an American style used for cutting rough wood on the farm (figure 111b).

Saws with metal frames include the coping saw and the fret saw (figures 112 and 113), although in the nineteenth century a fret saw was what today would be called a pad saw (figure 116).

Both these were made for curved work, the coping saw for 'coping' the parts of a scribed joint, or removing the waste between dovetails, and the fret saw for intricate curves in, for instance, jigsaw puzzles; foot-powered machines for fret work were very popular in the first half of the twentieth century. Framed saws much larger than those above were, as in continental Europe, preferred in some British trades for specialised joinery work such as chair or wheel making.

110. This turning saw has a wooden 'clack' (the Sheffield word for the uvula) to strain the cord and put the blade in tension.

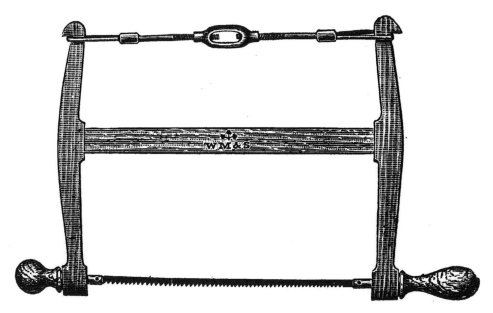

111a. The 1903 William Marples catalogue version has a metal straining rod.

111b. American-style buck saw from a
catalogue of 1911.

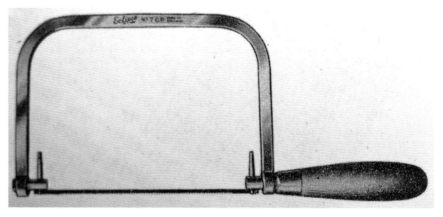

112. A coping saw from the 1950s; the blade can be rotated within the frame; cheaper types had a
fixed blade.

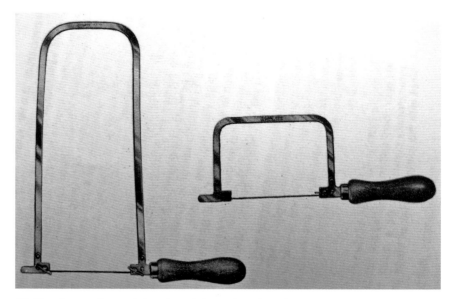

113. Two fret saws, long and short framed, dating from the 1950s.

Other Short Saws

Only the most common types can be considered here; 'How to Find Out More' on p. 88 lists other sources of information.

Compass, or Keyhole, Saws
Narrow-bladed, with an open handle (more than one design can be found), and often with a thick toothed edge which tapered sharply to the back, in order to work round the necessary sharp curves. The narrowness of the blades made them vulnerable to bending and breaking.

Grafting and Table Saws
These are difficult or impossible to tell apart, and the reasons for their names are also unclear. They had an open handle and a narrow blade (but wider than a compass saw); small ones, with blades 10–14 inches long, were often included in cheap tool chests or DIY collections (see figures 139–141). The table saw (the origin of the name is in doubt) was usually longer, with a blade up to 28 inches.

Nests of Saws
These were intended for the occasional user, who might have slight use for each type, or a tradesman who worked in more than one material, but would find it an advantage to have only one handle for the three or four blades. The illustration shows the older pattern of screws to change the blades, but later the fastenings were the same kind of quick-release-handled nut as on modern bicycle wheels. The illustration in figure 114 has three blades, described as fret, compass and table.

Salt Saws
The only saws, also having an open handle, with a blade not of steel, but of zinc, or copper; both metals were resistant to the corrosion caused by cutting the blocks of salt which at one time were supplied for large kitchens.

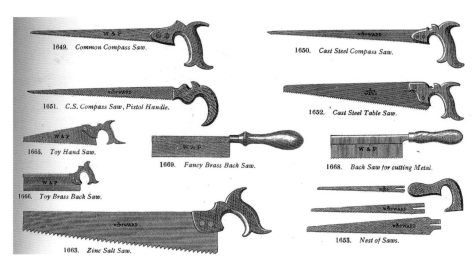

114. A Sheffield firm's 1911 catalogue showing different types of short saw.

115. A salt saw with a zinc blade; the simple handle shows the tool's utilitarian function.

Pad Saws

These came in two parts; one was the handle, usually of wood, which was sometimes expensive ebony or rosewood and strictly called a saw pad. The other part was the adjustable narrow blade, secured by one or two set screws in the handle. Later models had metal handles, with blades that could be for cutting wood or metal.

Floorboard Saws

A distinctively shaped saw, first made only in the 1920s, with a blade 10 to 12 inches long, used by tradesmen who needed to cut across a floorboard without damaging its neighbour. The main cutting edge was heavily convex, and the teeth were carried round on to the back for a short distance (not by all makers). The handle of the Roberts & Lee brand was also distinctive. Versions cut down by users from hand saws are quite common.

Turkish, or Monkey, Saws

Not commonly found, but so distinctive as to be worth describing. Made by Sheffield saw makers for markets in the Middle East and beyond, where woodworkers used a saw that cut on the pull stroke; hence the teeth pointed backwards. The shape of the blade and the handle were unique.

116. A beechwood saw pad; a so-called improved model had one set screw only.

117. Saw pads were also sold with a single fixed blade; in the nineteenth century (with a narrower blade) this would have been called a fret saw.

118. The usual pattern of floorboard saw, made about 1970.

119. Floorboard saw made by Roberts & Lee in about 1960.

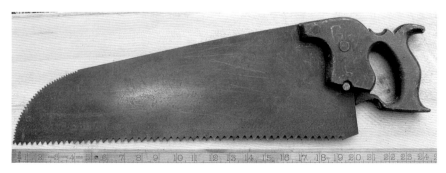

120. Homemade floorboard saw converted from a hand saw of about 1880.

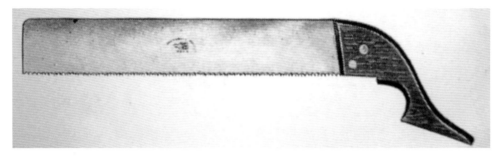

121. A Turkish saw, from a catalogue of 1950.

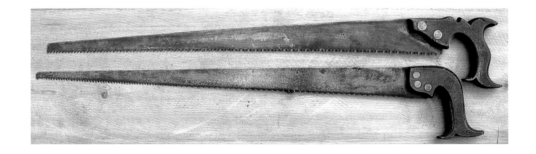

Above and left: **122a, 122b.** A table saw and a Turkish saw, both of the nineteenth century; the close up shows the difference in tooth pattern.

Staircase (Stair builder's or Grooving) Saws
The British saw industry did not advertise these for sale, but probably made them, chiefly for export. They were a fairly simple tool, and many examples are probably the result of a joiner's own making; it was usual for the teeth to cut on the pull stroke. American and continental European makers listed them.

Surgical Saws
Being largely owned nowadays by hospitals, they are not usually preserved or handed down to successor users in the way that woodworking tools were. In the nineteenth century surgeons often bought and maintained their own instruments; as surgeons were fewer in number than woodworkers, their saws are much less often found. Nineteenth-century surgical saws are usually easy to identify from their blade shape and the design and material of the handle, which was very often ivory or ebony. There were many other designs made for different types of surgery; it is probably easier to identify them by investigating the name on the saw, usually that of a dealer in surgical instruments in London.

123. A German grooving, or stair builder's saw, made about 1970.

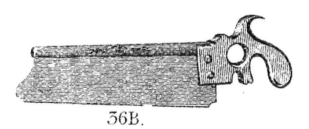

36B.

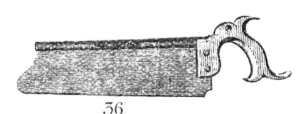

124. Two designs of surgical saw from a catalogue of 1880; the shape of the toe is characteristic.

36.

Large, or 'Long' Saws

The Sheffield saw trade denoted any saw with a blade over 30 inches in length as a long saw. There were several kinds for different purposes. The longest and most ancient in form were the two-man cross cuts, also called felling or falling saws; production lengths of 4–8 feet were standard from the earliest days of the British industry.

The one-man cross cut was an invention of the second half of the nineteenth century, and could also be used by two men if the second, upright handle was fixed at the end. All these large saws could be made with many different tooth-forms, sawyers all over the world having their own favourite for their local timbers.

Pit saws, intended, as the name implies, for use in the saw pit where timber was converted to regular shapes for carpentry and joinery, were either open-bladed with a turned wooden handle at each end, or framed. Note that saws used in coal mines were called miners' saws, not pit saws. In most countries other than Britain the work was done on raised trestles, using either framed or open-bladed saws.

The term whip saw is a very old one, and seems to have been applied to all open-bladed long saws; the blades always tapered from one end to the other, but some were much narrower than others if they were intended for sawing felloes for wheels, or staves for casks. Of course any saw that started with a wide blade becomes narrower with sharpening.

Large saws were also manufactured for cutting stone, not wood. One type closely resembled the one-man cross cut, another a wide-bladed two-man cross cut, and others simply a hardened steel plate without teeth that would run in a cut in the stone, lubricated by a stream of water and an abrasive, with power supplied by machine or the human arm.

125. A two-man cross-cut saw with a 4-foot blade made in about 1930; as figure 50 shows, this model is still in production.

126. A one-man cross-cut saw from a catalogue of 1920; there are two alternative positions for the upright handle.

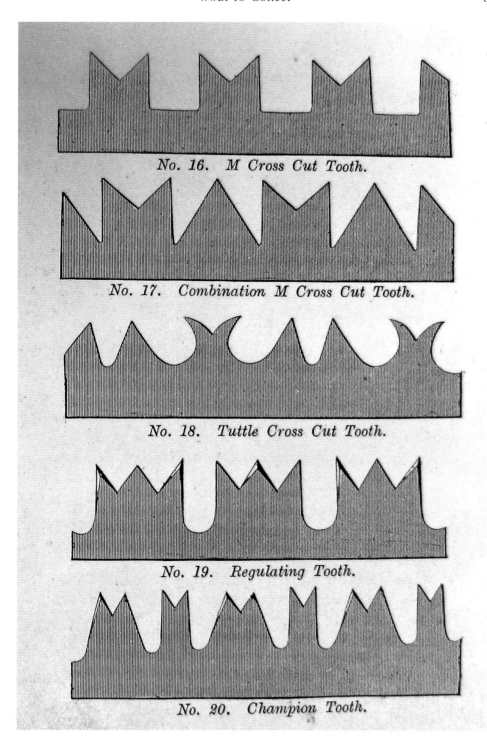

127. Tooth forms for cross-cut saws from a 1915 catalogue.

128. Timber conversion using a frame saw; note that the saw dust is not falling on the bottom sawyer, although it might if there was a high wind.

Above: **129.** Timber conversion on trestles (Norway, 2010); the sawyers are using a nineteenth-century Sheffield saw.

Right: **130.** Long saws of six kinds, from the catalogue of a Sheffield saw firm, 1890; saws of this kind were in earlier times called whip saws.

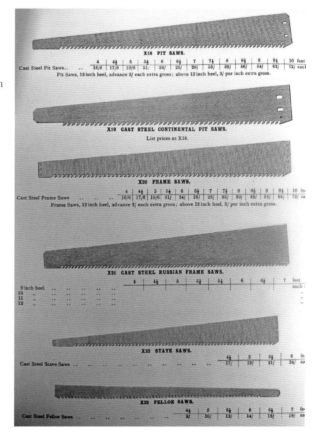

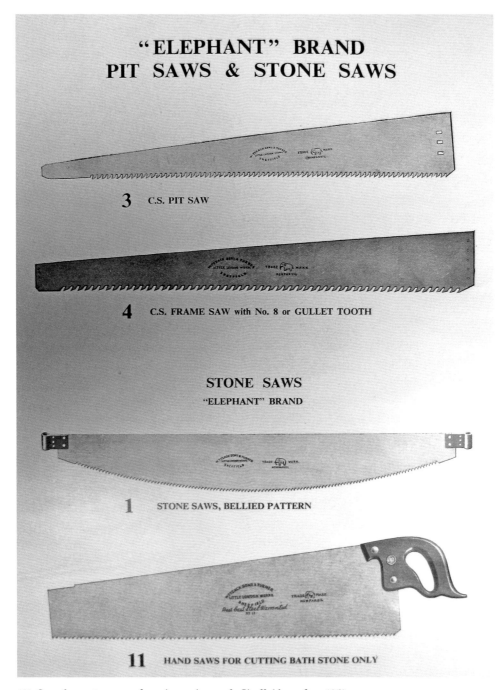

"ELEPHANT" BRAND
PIT SAWS & STONE SAWS

3   C.S. PIT SAW

4   C.S. FRAME SAW with No. 8 or GULLET TOOTH

STONE SAWS
"ELEPHANT" BRAND

1   STONE SAWS, BELLIED PATTERN

11   HAND SAWS FOR CUTTING BATH STONE ONLY

131. Saws for cutting stone, from the catalogue of a Sheffield saw firm, 1950.

Tools Related to Saws and Saw Making

Saw Setting Tools
Setting the teeth of a saw, that is, bending the top third of every other tooth slightly to one side, and the alternate ones the other way, is essential for efficient cutting through wood, enabling the teeth to create a cut that is fractionally wider than the thickness of the rest of the blade, a fact noted by saw makers and users since Roman times. The bending can be done by striking a blow with a special hammer, by the action of a piston in a kind of jig, or by a special type of pliers. Saw manufacturers employed men whose job was to do little else than saw setting, and they always used the hammer method; their speed and skill in aiming accurately at a saw tooth tip that might be a triangle with sides of about 1 mm could not be matched even by joiners who tuned their saws once a week at the most (see figure 49). To make the job easier, saw-setting devices of multitudinous forms have been devised, with a website giving many links and much information (see How to Find Out More, p. 89).

Other tools used in saw making and repairing included hammers of various shapes and sizes, anvils large and small, straight edges and different kinds of clamps and vices used to hold the saws for sharpening.

132. A few of the many saw-setting pliers in the Ken Hawley Collection, Sheffield.

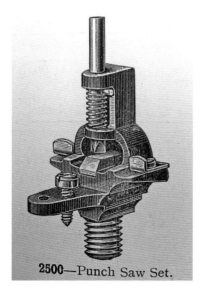

2500—Punch Saw Set.

Left: **133.** A punch saw set, from a Sheffield firm's catalogue of 1903.

Below: **134.** Another design of punch saw set from the same catalogue.

2502—Punch Saw Set.

Right: **135.** A punch saw set of the late nineteenth century, designed to be fastened to a work bench.

Below: **136.** A small saw-setting anvil with four different sized faces; number 1, as shown, has the smallest radius for the smallest tooth size.

137. A saw setting hammer with two different sized faces, this one for numbers 1 and 2, the narrowest.

138. A saw maker's straight edge, used during manufacture or repair to test a blade for 'tension' (see page 000).

Tool Chests and Kits

Several firms put together a collection of tools, some marketed as 'starter' kits for young people, some for occasional household repairs, and some for a DIY or even more serious tool user. The practice has a long history, and in the eighteenth and nineteenth centuries, when wealthy men engaged in woodwork as a genteel hobby, these chests were made of the finest timbers in beautiful cabinets, containing up to several dozen tools of all kinds.

Compared to these, this 1930s version in a brown cardboard attaché case seems very humble (figure 141).

139. The most expensive tool chest in Marples' 1903 catalogue: note that it is described as a handsome piece of furniture.

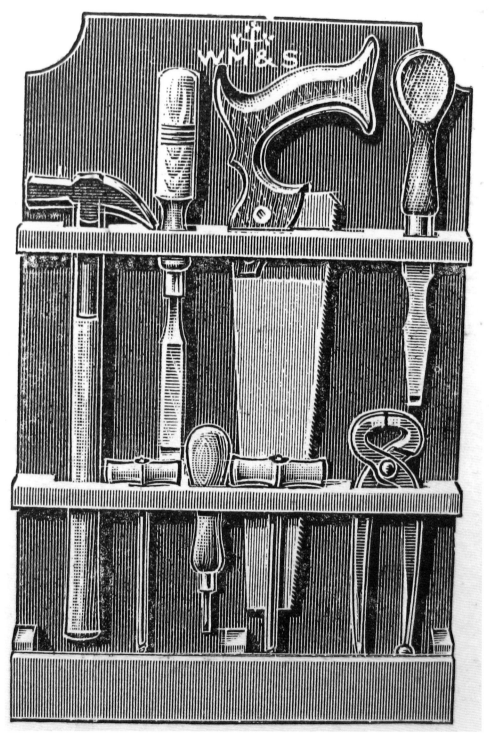

140. The cheapest tool rack in Marples' 1903 catalogue.

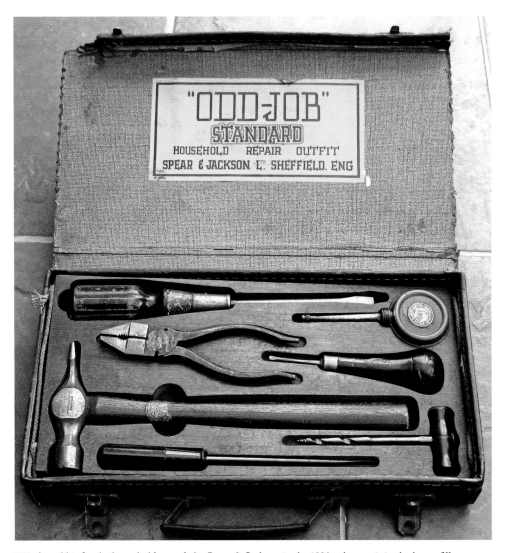

141. A tool kit for the householder made by Spear & Jackson in the 1930s; the saw is in the lower fill.

Other Collectables Related to Saws

Here again, collectors can decide for themselves whether they are attracted by something related to saws – one person might go for the many different designs of portable saw bench, such as the Workmate, while another could concentrate on saw sets, or some of the many small machines used in the saw-making industries before automation: the list that follows is far from comprehensive.

Advertising and other publicity material
Scores of firms advertised in the trade directories of the nineteenth and twentieth centuries, the directories themselves being a major source of information about manufacturers.

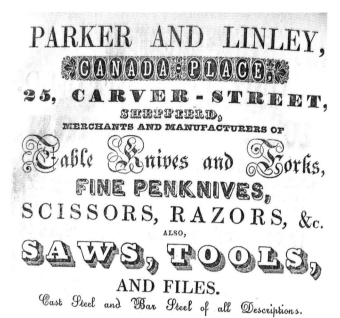

142. A saw firm's advertisement of 1845; the cutlery would have been bought in ('factored').

143. A saw firm's advertisement of 1864; bandsaws were a comparatively recent introduction.

There is a brisk trade in out-of-copyright reproductions of these advertisements, often nicely mounted, as the directories themselves are usually not cheap.

Manufacturers also made their presence known in trade magazines such as *The Ironmonger*, or *The Illustrated Carpenter and Builder* (figure 144).

Advertisements were, and of course continue to be, found in woodworking magazines such as *The Woodworker*, first published over 100 years ago, but only the larger firms could afford to use special means of publicity, such as this set of playing cards, a small tin of sticking plasters, or a calendar (figures 145–147).

3UILDER.   [MAY 11, 1888.

E. DUCKENFIELD'S
Registered IMPROVED
DOVETAIL AND TENON SAWS.

The forward POINT of these Saws being BROADER than at the HEEL, makes them HANG better, HEAVIER at the POINT, CUT DEEPER, keep in the CUT more EASILY than any Saws ever produced. This is a valuable consideration with Carpenters, Coachmakers, Pattern-makers, and all who use them.

The EXTRA WIDTH also compensates for the HARD WEAR to which this part is subject, and enables it to be THOROUGHLY EFFICIENT for a much longer time than is the case with Saws of the ordinary Pattern.

The Saws are made of the Best Material and Workmanship, and will be exchanged if not satisfactory.

Brass Back Saws, 14in., 6s. each.
Two Brass Back Saws, 14in., for 11s.
Brass Back Dovetail Saws, 10in., 4s. 6d. each.
Two Brass Back Dovetail Saws, 10in., for 8s. 6d.

CARRIAGE PAID.
Iron Backs, 1s. each less.

E. DUCKENFIELD,
MANUFACTURER AND PATENTEE.

144. The only two recorded examples of this saw show the mark of the Sheffield firm of Garlick, founded in 1864; saws with this name are still being made (see also figure 147).

145.

146. As the largest and oldest (founded 1760) Sheffield firm of saw makers, Spear & Jackson produced a wide range of advertising materials.

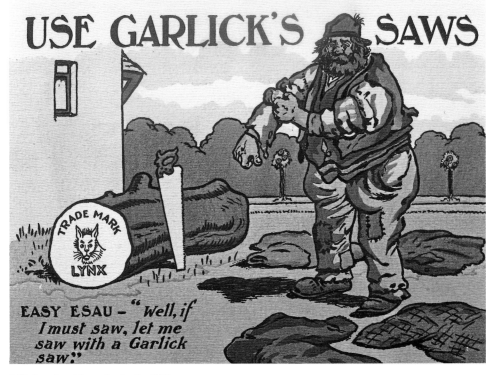

147. An advertising calendar for 1978.

The most eye-catching of all publicity material was the display case of tools, and it is fortunate for posterity that these cases, originally few in number, are more likely to be preserved than comparatively ephemeral material. They were expensive to put together, but makers everywhere could draw on the resources of a large and flourishing branch of cabinet case making (devoted mainly to canteens and boxes for the cutlery trades). Perhaps the most common reason for making them was to be part of a display at a trade show, or in the premises of a large retailer. It was a common practice to include miniature versions of products; although few in number, these objects sometimes turn up for sale today.

Casting one's net still wider, there are many other emanations of saws, as a comb, a lighter, a paper knife, an eraser, even as a brand of matches; the tin sawyers from an early twentieth-century German maker is just one toy among many others.

Nor did the tobacco or picture postcard industries neglect saws and sawing, as seen on pages 77 and 78.

148. A display case by Copley of London from the 1851 Great Exhibition.

149. Some of the many ways in which saws were used for novelties or toys, this one a comb made by an American firm.

150. Eraser.

152. A lighter.

153. A paper knife.

154. A box of matches.

155. One of a series of postcards of 'Russian types' of about 1900, this shows timber being planked; it is very likely that their saws had been made in Sheffield.

156. A cigarette card from the 1930s; on the reverse is an attempted explanation of the saw nib which, like most, is not correct.

Catalogues

The catalogues of many small firms were produced but have not survived. Those of the larger and longer lived are not hard to find, particularly in reprinted form; naturally the further back the collector tries to go, the rarer and more expensive they become. There is a very large collection of catalogues, not saw makers' alone, in the Ken Hawley Tool Collection in Sheffield, where they can be consulted (see How to Find Out More).

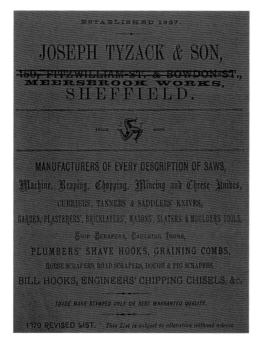

157. The cover of Joseph Tyzack's 1879 catalogue; their three-leg trademark was adopted after the owner made a trip to the Isle of Man.

Invoices and Bills

Often both attractive and informative, they gave nineteenth-century printers the opportunity to let themselves go in the way that they did with advertising in trade directories.

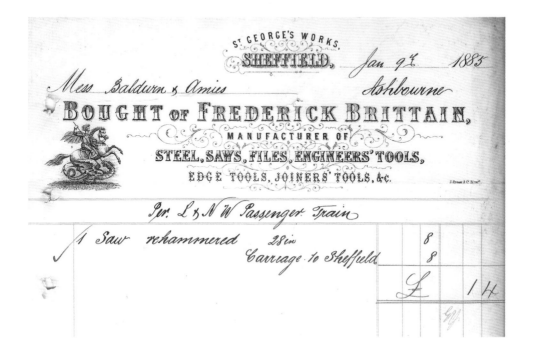

Above: **158.** The naming of Groves' Beehive Works helped to suggest the firm's industriousness.

Right: **159.** Taylor Brothers produced more brands of saws than any other saw firm.

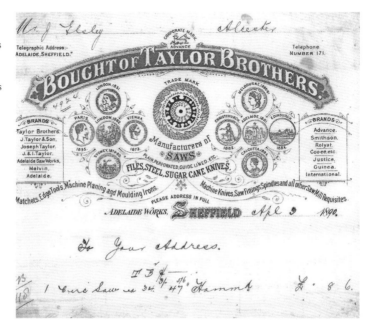

How to Look After a Collection

Once again, the answers to this problem depend on what is being collected and the conditions of its storage: big old pit saws that are often found covered in rust can usually be safely left, once cleaned and well oiled, in a barn or dry shed, whereas paper materials need to be dry and indoors.

All objects, of whatever size and material, must have an initial inspection to decide whether any cleaning is needed. There is an element of personal taste to this decision, the main criteria being whether the object is in a stable state or not, i.e. liable to deteriorate if left alone, and how precious it is, in absolute or personal terms.

The next level of decisions is again personal, and depends on whether the owner thinks the tool should resemble its original state, whether it should be restored to being useable, or whether it should simply be stabilised and kept for reference (and admiration by oneself and others, of course). The principle to be kept in mind at all times is to avoid doing anything irreversible, so that caution is always necessary.

Cleaning and preserving paper or card material is for museums and archives a highly specialised task, with trained staff using high quality museum-grade materials at all times. For the interested amateur this level of permanent preservation is seldom the aim, and simply getting rid of surface dust and dirt by brushing and perhaps a soft eraser will usually suffice (specialist advisory sources are listed in How to Find Out More, p. 85).

What to do about *metal objects* depends on the metal; brass or bronze tools may tarnish, but do not decay badly in the same way as ferrous metals. Not long ago the back alone of a brass back saw was found at the bottom of the English Channel, the result of a shipwreck in 1855; it was in perfect condition, the blade and handle having disappeared, apart from tiny scraps of rusty steel trapped within it. The treatment of ferrous metals is altogether more problematical, and there have been many methods published which a search online will throw up. My own treatment of saws, which is included on p. 91, aims at restoring the tool to something approaching its original state, unless its corrosion is too far gone, and only if doing so preserves original features, such as an etched mark: my reasons for using these procedures are that I collect saws either for use, or for a reference collection in a museum, but others with different aims for their collection will have different criteria. Once cleaned, the tool can be saved from further corrosion by the use of a proprietary product; my preference is for Renaissance Wax (see appendix). It is worth noting that if saws have to be stored in less than perfect conditions they can be preserved from damage by coating liberally with linseed oil: it is cheap, readily available, and even when hardened after many years can be removed without much difficulty, although the saw would be no use for cutting wood until the blade has been freed from its sticky coating.

Housing a collection will depend on the number of objects and the space available. A few saws can hang up to four or five deep on a stout dowel, or the person with skills on the cabinet-making level may want to construct a cupboard with a separate rack for each saw. The combined Ken Hawley and Simon Barley saw collections (figure 1) are in a severely limited space for their 2,000 saws, so much so that about 500 are off site entirely; the hand and back saws are housed in racks of ten, with the longer saws hung singly or (unsatisfactorily) standing on the floor against a wall. Much more elegant solutions have been found.

160. A beautifully made saw rack; this design is infinitely expansible, and can be adapted to hold many kinds of saws.

Where to Go to Collect Saws

The attractions of today's internet and its online auctions are undeniable, not least because the tools advertised there can be sold to and from anywhere in the world. The number and range of saws and saw-related objects on sale on any one day on eBay alone is usually in the thousands, and the standard of presentation is usually very high. Most saws bought in this way can be relied on to be what they purport to be, and the ways of redressing grievances are well defined and effective. British saws for sale in the United States are often export models which for obvious reasons are harder to find here.

There is, however, little to beat an old-fashioned auction, where everything is there to be picked up, handled and personally appraised; the largest real-time auctions now also offer the chance of bidding online. At these events tool collectors assemble not only to buy, but perhaps also to meet friends, talk things over, and buy and sell at the tables surrounding the auction itself. Specialist auctioneers of tools in Britain include David Stanley Auctions, with six auctions per year (two international) and Tony Murland, who holds two international per year.

There are several retail establishments specialising in old tools, shops run by enthusiasts, whose knowledge can usually ensure that what they are selling is authentic; most sell new as well as used tools. A usefully comprehensive list is at http://taths.org.uk/tools-and-trades/notes/140-rn-03-uk-old-tool-dealers.

Many antique shops which do not specialise in tools often have a few for sale, but my experience is that their lack of familiarity in the field makes them overprice some of their wares, at the same time as underappreciating others. At the other end of the scale, saws and other collectibles can sometimes be found in the smarter ambience of an antique fair, with prices to match; the antique fairs at Newark-on-Trent are described as the biggest in Europe.

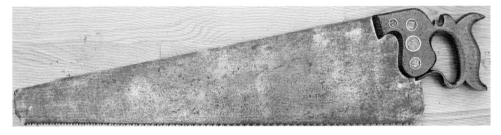

161. A saw made in the nineteenth century for US export (see also figures 162 and 163).

Above: **162.** The locomotive is obviously American.

Left: **163.** Multiple medallion screws were almost never fitted to saws sold in Britain, but often for the US market (see also figure 75).

How to Find Out More

Organisations

The Tools and Trades History Society (TATHS) has a nationwide and international membership, with a quarterly newsletter, an occasional scholarly journal (*Tools and Trades*), an active website (www.taths.org.uk/), and regional groups with frequent meetings and visits where members share knowledge, experience (particularly about preserving a collection) and tools. There is an annual three-day conference, held at different places such as Birmingham, Sheffield, Ironbridge, Chatham (the historic dockyard) and others that can offer visits to special museums and collections. Joining such an active and knowledgeable group has many attractions that nothing else can match.

In the United States there are several similar bodies, notably the Early American Industries Association and the Mid-Western Tool Collectors' Association, both of which, with a much larger membership than TATHS, produce quarterly publications that sometimes include information about British tools.

Museums

The largest collection of saws in one place in Britain is at the Ken Hawley Collection, housed at Kelham Island Industrial Museum, Sheffield (http://www. hawleytoolcollection.com); this collection of tools of all kinds was started by the late Ken Hawley, who lived and worked all his life in Sheffield. With his knowledge and his connections with local industry, he put together an unparalleled number of tools, the tools used to make these tools, the business documents of many of them when, during the period 1960–90, so many of them closed down, and a huge number of tool catalogues. His great interest was in how tools were made, and in his search for this information he saved many saws in the process of being made, as well as unique tools the manufacturing tradesmen used (figures 164–167).

Ken's collection has been supplemented by the growing Simon Barley Saw Collection; the combined total now approaches 2,000 saws, the overall aim being eventually to create a reference collection of British saws.

Like all museums, the Ken Hawley Collection is obliged from lack of space to keep most of its objects in store, but with notice these are all available for inspection by the public; information on access is on the website http://www.hawleytoolcollection. com; contact can also be made by post to The Hawley Collection, Kelham Island Museum, Alma Street, Sheffield, South Yorkshire, England, S3 8RY, or by phone to 0114 2010770.

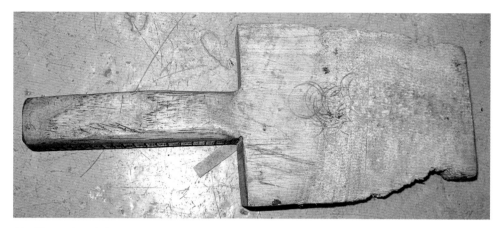

164. This tool, made by its user, was called a bat and was used to drive the blade tightly into the steel or brass back.

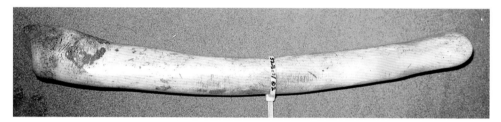

165. The best quality saw handles were burnished with a bone, probably here the rib of a cow, to close the grain of the wood.

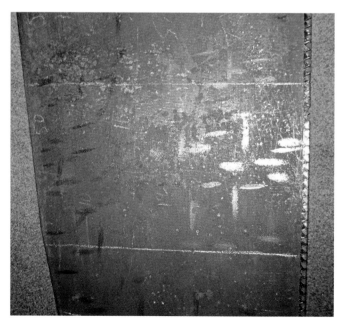

166. A hand saw plate at an early stage of manufacture: it has not yet been polished and shows the hammer marks of the saw smith.

167. This upright log of lignum vitae (a 'stake') has a squared face for the final light smithing ('blocking') of the blade; also visible are two types of saw smithing hammers, one a so-called dog head, the other the twist face pattern.

Other places with saws and saw-making materials include the Science Museum (www.sciencemuseum.org.uk) in London, although much of its collections related to saws and saw making is in storage. Another major collection of tools is at the Weald and Downland Open Air Museum (www.wealddown.co.uk) at Singleton, West Sussex; access to the saws may need a special request. In Wales St Fagans National History Museum in Cardiff is an even larger open-air museum with its main emphasis on recreated buildings and rural industries; some saws are included in these (www.museumwales.ac.uk/stfagans). There are many other local and folk museums in Britain which have a few saws among their collections of historic tools, but in a limited search of them I have not so far found anything which is not in the Sheffield collections. The contents of the technical, industrial and historical museums of other nations doubtless include some British saws, but I do have any knowledge of them beyond what an internet search would tell me. There are a great many well-informed private collectors of British saws in the USA and other countries whose private collections add to our knowledge; many of them contribute to the website www.backsaw.net.

Reading List: Books

Not all of these are in print, and in those with tool price guides there is inevitably information which is out of date; some are only partly devoted to saws. The second one in the list is the largest and most comprehensive, but does not include prices.

Barley, Simon, 'White saws, probably the best in the world', *EAIA Chronicle*, 68, No. 3 (2015) pp. 93–110.

Barley, Simon, *British Saws and Saw Makers from 1660* (Gloucester: Choir Press, 2014).

Gaynor, James M. and Nancy L. Hagedorn, *Tools: Working Wood in Eighteenth-Century America* (Williamsburg: Colonial Williamsburg Foundation, 1993).

Gaynor, James M. (ed.), *Eighteenth-Century Woodworking Tools: papers presented at a Tool Symposium, May 19–22, 1994* (Williamsburg: Colonial Williamsburg Foundation, 1997).

Goodman, W. L., *The History of Woodworking Tools* (London: G. Bell, 1964).

Grimshaw, Robert, *Grimshaw on Saws* (1880, reprinted edition, Morristown, New Jersey: Astragal Press, n.d.).

Jones, P. d'A. and E. N. Simons, *Story of the Saw* (Manchester, Birmingham & London: Newman Neame, 1961).

Murland, Tony, *Antique Tool Value Guide* (Suffolk: PJ Print, 2007).

Rees, Jane and Mark, *Tools: a Guide for Collectors* (Second edition, Needham Market: Roy Arnold, 1999).

Salaman, R. A., *Dictionary of Woodworking Tools c. 1700-1970* (revised edition, London, Allen & Unwin, 1989).

Schaffer, E. L. C. and D. McConnell, *Hand-saw makers of Britain: A Checklist of Hand-saw Makers* (Rockford, Illinois: Osage Press, 2005).

Spear & Jackson Ltd, *Concerning Handsaws* (a small booklet produced in several editions during the twentieth century; the firm also put out other booklets on saws).

The Handsaw Catalog Collection: A Select Compilation of the Four Leading Manufacturers (1910–1919) (Mendham, New Jersey: Astragal Press, 1994).

Reading List: magazines

Most magazines about woodworking from time to time include articles about hand tools, and, less often, saws. The following list of monthlies published in Britain may not be complete, and there are others published in the United States and elsewhere.

The Woodworker, Woodworking Crafts, Furniture and Cabinet Making and *Good Woodworking.*

Other sources of information

For saw sets there is an extremely comprehensive and authoritative website: http://members.acmenet.net/, called by its originator Mark Conley 'The Saw Set Collector's Resource'.

An excellent article on 'Looking after Tools' has been prepared by TATHS; it can be accessed at http://taths.org.uk/tools-and-trades/notes/48-conservation-notes/-introduction. TATHS is also developing a series of advice notes on looking after tools (see its website). A web search would pick up several other articles of a similar nature. There are a great many proprietary products for cleaning metals of all kinds; users should always be cautious.

Appendix: Cleaning a Saw

The tool in this demonstration of cleaning is a 12-inch iron back saw of about 1890, marked Armitage (a Sheffield maker) and London (a word denoting quality).

It was grossly rusty and sad, with apparently quite deep pitting in places, and it took about 30 minutes of work to achieve these results, which sharp eyes will see have not entirely eliminated the worst of the rust at the toe end of the blade.

I used dry garnet paper (obtainable from internet sites, but rarely from high street tool and material suppliers) rather than papers gritted with aluminium oxide because garnet, a natural mineral, has a hardness less than most steels, but greater than rust, so that although you might put scratches into the steel with the coarsest grades (60 or 80 grit), these are easy to get rid of using the finer grades (120, 180 or even 240 grit in succession). Light rust doesn't need much below 120 grit. Aluminium oxide is in my opinion too hard, and will permanently scratch the steel, but I know that other people are happy to use the finer grades with a lubricant like WD40. Some collectors take the handle off, but this is usually a bad idea when the screws are the flat kind that need a forked screwdriver, as they are nigh on impossible to replace neatly. Without the handle it is then possible to put the blade into an electrolytic bath to be de-rusted, the result being a peculiarly horrible dead surface, admittedly rust free, but also devoid of any trace of the original polished finish. Another similar cleaning material is molasses, immersion in which will do the same job as electrolysis, but very slowly. And if you have an angle grinder, please don't let me see the results of your using it on a saw (I have, alas).

There are three awkward areas on a saw: one is the part next to the handle, where I wrap the abrasive paper round a small flat piece of wood and with that get up close to the wood. The second is the teeth themselves, which respond pretty well to a stiff brass (not steel) wire brush. I also cautiously follow the line of the saw handle with the same brush, aiming to avoid leaving scratches in that shape on the steel. The third tricky area is the maker's etched mark on the blade. The process of etching varied with

168. Armitage saw before cleaning.

169. Handle of an Armitage back saw before cleaning.

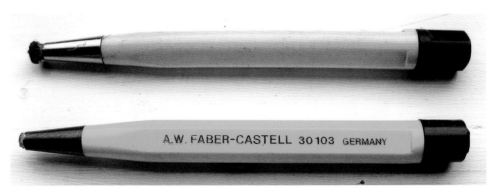

170. A Faber pen, for which refills are available, and miniature wire brush.

makers and with time, some being so deep they almost seem like a mark applied with a punch, and some so frail that even slight abrasion with very fine grit means a quick goodbye to ever reading it. Just start very carefully, as indeed you always should if you don't know what may be under the rust. If it's a mark struck with a punch, there is much more scope to be vigorous (a miniature wire brush is good); a Faber Castell glass eraser pen is good for more gentle work on brass. Both should be kept well clear of an etched or printed mark.

Finally it's usually best to apply something to stop the rust advancing. Some form of wax is popular, and in museums the favourite is Renaissance Wax, which is formulated to do no damage. I apply it with a nylon kitchen pan scourer to the wood, and with a rag or my fingers to the metal. I've found that it's only very seldom that a saw can't be brought to something like this one, unless the plate is very pitted and corroded.

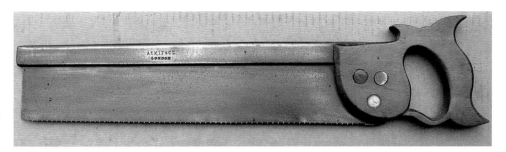

171. Armitage saw after cleaning.

WILLIAM H. ARMITAGE,

MANUFACTURER OF

SAWS,

Gold Coloured SILVER STEEL and HARD COMPOSITION

DOCTORS,

LADIES' STEEL BUSKS, &c.,

BURNT TREE LANE WORKS,

SHEFFIELD.

172. An Armitage advertisement from a directory of 1849. A 'doctor' here was a type of cast steel blade used in the textile industries; making them was allied to making saw blades.

Saw Nomenclature and Glossary

Most of the terms used to describe the parts of saws are explained or illustrated in the text. The two diagrams complete this explanation; they have been modified with permission from an article on nomenclature by Ray Gardiner on the website www. backsaw.net.

Taper grinding produced a blade that was thinner at the back (the edge opposite to the teeth) by 4–6 thousandths of an inch, facilitating the passage of the saw through the wood. The cheapest saws had no taper, and were flat ground.

Teeth *per inch* gives an indication of how quickly the saw will cut; the term points per inch was the one saw makers used, and is always one less than the number of teeth. After about 1880 this number was often stamped on the blade at the heel of hand saws (not back saws).

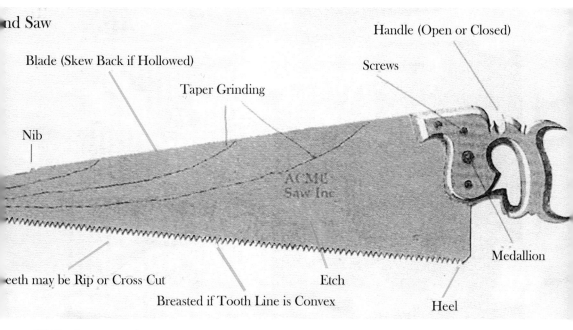

173. Hand saw nomenclature.

Handsaw Handle

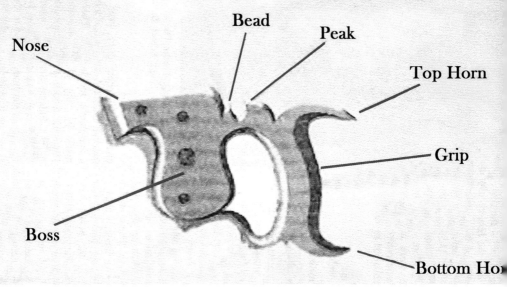

174. Saw handle nomenclature.